THE GIANT OF THE SKY

By Cynthia Rider

Illustrated by Rob Hefferan

CAMBRIDGE
UNIVERSITY PRESS

A lion went to hunt in a deep, dark wood.
He went past a tent and he smelt something good.

Then he felt a big BUMP on the top of his head, and just as he did, a gruff voice said,

"I am the GIANT OF THE SKY,
and what I like best is a Crusty Lion Pie."

"I must run past this giant as fast as I can!"
Then away from the wood, the big lion ran.

A tiger went to hunt in the deep, dark wood.
He went past the tent and he smelt something good.

Then he felt a big THUMP on the back of his head, and just as he did, a gruff voice said,

"I am the GIANT OF THE SKY,
and my very best treat is a Tiger to eat!"

"I must run. I must dash. I just don't trust this pest!"
Then the tiger ran fast to his den in the west.

An elephant went to the deep, dark wood.
He went past the tent and he smelt something good.

Then he felt a little PING on the front of his head, and just as he did, a gruff voice said,

"I am the GIANT OF THE SKY,
and what I want most is an Elephant on Toast."

The elephant looked up, and he said, “Dear me! There's a giant with a catapult sitting in this tree!”

"There is," said the giant, who was really very small.
"I'm the Giant of the Sky and I scared you all!"

The elephant waved and went on his way.
So the Giant of the Sky put his catapult away.

Then the Giant of the Sky came down from the tree, and he said, “Are those beans on toast for me?”